**W9-ALL-901**

# WORLD BOOK'S
# LIBRARY OF NATURAL DISASTERS
# HEAT WAVES

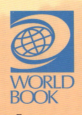

**WORLD BOOK**

a Scott Fetzer company
Chicago
**www.worldbookonline.com**

World Book, Inc.
233 N. Michigan Avenue
Chicago, IL 60601
U.S.A.

For information about other World Book publications, visit our Web site at
**http://www.worldbookonline.com** or call **1-800-WORLDBK (967-5325).**

For information about sales to schools and libraries, call **1-800-975-3250 (United States)**;
**1-800-837-5365 (Canada).**

2008 revised printing

**Library of Congress Cataloging-in-Publication Data**

Heat waves.
      p. cm. -- (World Book's library of natural disasters)
    Summary: "A discussion of a major type of natural
disaster, including descriptions of some of the most
severe heat waves; explanations of these phenomena,
what causes them, and where they occur; and
information about how to prepare for and survive these
forces of nature. Features include an activity, glossary,
list of resources, and index"--Provided by publisher.
    Includes bibliographical references and index.
    ISBN 978-0-7166-9807-4
    1. Heat waves (Meteorology)--Juvenile literature.
2. Natural disasters--Juvenile literature.
I. World Book, Inc.
QC981.8.A5H43 2008
363.34'92--dc22
                              2007013710

World Book's Library of Natural Disasters
Set ISBN: 978-0-7166-9801-2

Printed in China
2 3 4 5 6 12 11 10 09 08

Editor in Chief: Paul A. Kobasa

Supplementary Publications
    Associate Director: Scott Thomas
    Managing Editor: Barbara A. Mayes

Editors: Jeff De La Rosa, Nicholas Kilzer,
    Christine Sullivan, Kristina A. Vaicikonis,
    Marty Zwikel

Researchers: Cheryl Graham, Jacqueline Jasek

Manager, Editorial Operations
    (Rights & Permissions): Loranne K. Shields

Graphics and Design
    Associate Director: Sandra M. Dyrlund
    Associate Manager, Design: Brenda B. Tropinski
    Associate Manager, Photography: Tom Evans
    Designer: Matt Carrington

Product development: Arcturus Publishing Limited
Writer: Neil Morris
Editors: Nicola Barber, Alex Woolf
Designer: Jane Hawkins
Illustrator: Stefan Chabluk

**Acknowledgments:**

AP Photo: 12 (Michel Euler), 13, 37 (Franck Prevel), 19, 21 (Beth A. Keiser), 22 (Associated Press).

Corbis: 4, 11, 40, 43 (Reuters), 7 (Rick D'Elia), 9 (Corbis), 17 (Marcelo del Pozo/ Reuters), 18 (Kusel Robert/ Corbis
    Sygma), 20 (P. Greer/ Chicago Tribune/ Corbis Sygma), 23, 32, 33 (Bettmann), 26 (Robert Dowling), 28 (David
    Gray/ Reuters), 29 (Claro Cortes IV/ Reuters), 31 (Chris Hocking/ epa), 34 (Jim Reed), 38 (Kimimasa Mayama/
    Reuters), 41 (China Photos/ Reuters), 42 (Hayden Roger Celestin/ epa).

The Detroit News: 24, 25.

Getty Images: 6 (Olivier Laban-Mattei/ AFP), 35 (Justin Sullivan), 36 (Patrick Lin/ AFP).

Knowledge Resource Centre, Department of Primary Industries, Victoria: 30.

NASA: 10 (Reto Stockli and Robert Simmon, NASA's Earth Observatory Team).

Science Photo Library: 14 (Paul Rapson), 15 (R. Mulvaney).

Superstock: cover/ title page (age fotostock).

# TABLE OF CONTENTS

**Glossary** There is a glossary of terms on pages 45-46. Terms defined in the glossary are in type **that looks like this** on their first appearance on any spread (two facing pages).

**Additional resources** Books for further reading and recommended Web sites are listed on page 47. Because of the nature of the Internet, some Web site addresses may have changed since publication. The publisher has no responsibility for any such changes or for the content of cited sources.

# WHAT IS A HEAT WAVE?

A heat wave is a period of very hot weather. We usually use the term *heat wave* when the temperature rises well above the normal level for a particular region and stays at the higher level for an extended period of time. For this reason, the definition of a heat wave varies around the world. A certain temperature might be thought normal in one place at a particular time of year. But the same temperature might be seen as very high in another part of the world. For example, a temperature of 86 °F (30 °C) is hot in the United Kingdom and some regions of the United States. If this temperature went on for more than a few days, it would be called a heat wave. But 86 °F is fairly normal in parts of Australia and the southern United States.

## Around the world

The **climate** varies around the world. Some places generally have more rain than others, and some have much higher temperatures. The following table shows the average temperature in different places around the world at different times. It is easy to see why someone in Khartoum, in the North African country of Sudan, might not call an average summer temperature of 90 °F (32.2 °C) a heat wave. But in Melbourne, Australia—where January is the height of summer—people might take a very different view.

Two men on a street in Islamabad use massive ice blocks to keep cool during a heat wave that hit Pakistan in June 2003. Temperatures reached 111 °F (44 °C).

## Defining a heat wave

In 1900, an American **meteorologist** defined a heat wave as "three or more consecutive days where the maximum shade temperature reaches 90 °F (32 °C)." This definition was used for the entire United States. Today, meteorologists understand that the definition does not work for all areas. For example, in northern California, with high average summer temperatures, the forecast office of the National Weather Service defines a heat wave as "three or more consecutive days where the temperature reaches 100 °F (38 °C)."

### HIGHEST TEMPERATURES EVER RECORDED

| Continent | Location | Temperature in °F (°C) | Year recorded |
|---|---|---|---|
| Africa | Al Aziziyah, Libya | 136 (58) | 1922 |
| North America | Death Valley, United States | 134 (57) | 1913 |
| Asia | Tirat Tsvi, Israel | 129 (54) | 1942 |
| Australia | Cloncurry, Australia | 128 (53) | 1889 |
| Europe | Seville, Spain | 122 (50) | 1881 |
| South America | Rivadavia, Argentina | 120 (49) | 1905 |
| Antarctica | Scott Coast | 59 (15) | 1974 |

*Source: U.S. National Climatic Data Center.*

**Average temperatures in °F (°C) on different continents:**

| Place, country | Continent | January | July | Year average |
|---|---|---|---|---|
| Johannesburg, South Africa | Africa | 69 (21) | 52 (11) | 61 (16) |
| Khartoum, Sudan | Africa | 75 (24) | 90 (32) | 86 (30) |
| Hong Kong, China | Asia | 62 (17) | 85 (29) | 75 (24) |
| Ulaanbaatar, Mongolia | Asia | –4 (–20) | 62 (17) | 31 (–1) |
| Darwin, Australia | Australia | 83 (28) | 77 (25) | 82 (28) |
| Melbourne, Australia | Australia | 68 (20) | 48 (9) | 58 (14) |
| Berlin, Germany | Europe | 31 (–1) | 65 (18) | 49 (9) |
| Malaga, Spain | Europe | 53 (12) | 76 (24) | 64 (18) |
| Houston, United States | N. America | 51 (11) | 84 (29) | 69 (21) |
| Toronto, Canada | N. America | 21 (–6) | 70 (21) | 46 (8) |
| Buenos Aires, Argentina | S. America | 75 (24) | 50 (10) | 62 (17) |
| Manaus, Brazil | S. America | 81 (27) | 81 (27) | 81 (27) |

*Source: Weatherbase.*

# DANGER TO HEALTH

A heat wave can cause serious health problems. Elderly people, infants, and people with long-term illnesses are especially at risk. If the problems are not treated quickly and effectively, extreme heat can kill people. According to the U.S. National Weather Service, nearly 20,000 people died in the United States from the effects of heat during the years 1936 to 1975. Experts say that these were direct casualties. Many more deaths might have been indirectly caused by hot weather. For example, people with weak hearts might have lived longer if they had not become overheated. More recently, researchers claimed that heat caused nearly 9,000 deaths in the United States from 1979 to 2002. During that period, more Americans died from extreme heat than from the combined effects of **hurricanes,** lightning, **tornadoes, floods,** and **earthquakes.**

**An aide helps an elderly man to drink a glass of water at a retirement home in Paris as temperatures soar during a heat wave in 2006. Elderly people are less able to adjust to the extreme temperatures experienced during heat waves.**

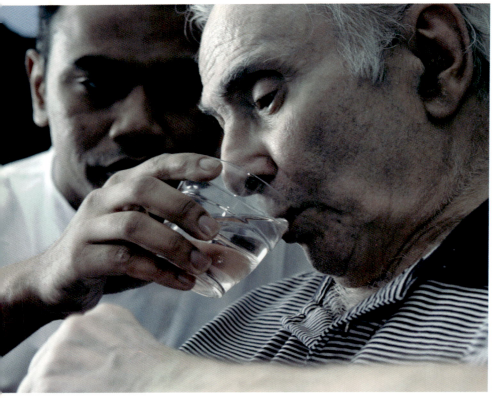

## Risks to older people

As people get older, their bodies are less able to adjust to high temperatures. Older people sweat less, so the body's natural cooling system does not work as effectively as it does for younger people. Some medical conditions, including **diabetes** and **high blood pressure,** add to the risk because they place the body's organs under additional stress. When the body cannot control its temperature because of extreme heat, a person may suffer from **hyperthermia.**

Hyperthermia occurs when the body temperature rises well above the normal level of 98.6 °F (37 °C). A temperature above 104 °F (40 °C) can cause the body to stop eliminating heat through the skin, so the person can no longer cool down.

## Dehydration

**Dehydration** is a condition in which the body loses too much water. In most cases, the body also loses salt. In severe cases, this condition can lead to a fast heartbeat, **low blood pressure,** shock, and even death. The risk from dehydration is particularly high in infants and elderly people.

## HEAT STROKE

**Heat stroke** (also called sunstroke) is a serious condition that can occur when the body becomes overheated. Doctors generally define heat stroke as a body temperature of 105 °F (40.6 °C). A person suffering heat stroke feels hot but cannot sweat. The skin becomes hot, dry, and red. The body temperature rises so high that it can cause damage to the brain if it is not lowered quickly. Heat stroke is very dangerous for people of all ages.

**Employees of the fire department in Phoenix, Arizona, hand out packs of water to residents during a heat wave in 2005. Lack of water can lead to a condition called dehydration.**

# WHAT CAUSES A HEAT WAVE?

Heat waves are generally created by areas of high **air pressure.** Weather experts call these **highs,** or **anticyclones.** Warm highs bring high temperatures and air that contains little moisture. These highs are massive **weather systems** that may affect a region for a long time. In the summer, a warm high sometimes stalls over North America, for example, causing a heat wave.

**The weather in the Northern Hemisphere is influenced by the movements of bodies of air called air masses. As the air masses move across great distances, they influence the weather below. Warm and humid maritime tropical air can cause heat waves in the summer.**

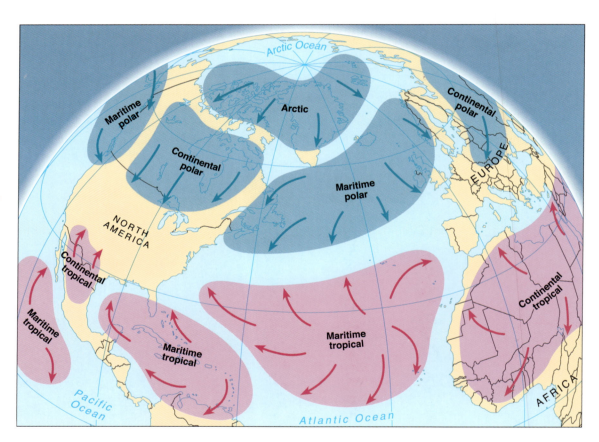

## Blocking high

Sometimes the weather seems to get stuck and remains the same for weeks or even months, preventing other weather systems from entering the area. **Meteorologists** call such a pattern *blocking.* In 1976, a **blocking high** lingered over the United Kingdom for the entire summer. Such an anticyclone often causes **droughts.**

## Humidity

The American National Red Cross defines a heat wave as "a prolonged period of excessive heat and **humidity.**" Humidity is the amount of **water vapor,** or moisture, in the air. Humidity varies according to the air's temperature and pressure. The warmer the air, the more water vapor it can hold. In many parts of the world, including the United States, heat waves are caused by anticyclones that also produce a high level of humidity. The amount of water vapor in the air compared with the total amount the air can hold is called **relative humidity.** Humidity affects our comfort and health. Our bodies cool off when we sweat, and the **perspiration evaporates.** When the temperature and the relative humidity are high, most people feel uncomfortable and "sticky" because their perspiration cannot evaporate easily.

### CORN STUDY

In 2002, researchers in Illinois who studied weather records going back 42 years found that heat waves in the region were increasingly linked to high humidity. They suspected that this change has been caused by an increase in the amount of corn grown in the state. Like all plants, corn gives off water vapor—about 4,000 gallons per acre (6,100 liters per hectare) daily. The researchers did not conclude that the corn had made the air hotter but that the corn had made the air more humid. They called this "a more dangerous breed of heat wave" because of the problems caused by high humidity.

**Fields of corn cover the rolling landscape of Illinois. Research has shown that such crops produce higher levels of humidity.**

# EUROPE, 2003

Scientists think that the summer of 2003 was probably the hottest in Europe for at least 500 years. A severe heat wave started in many places in June, lasted for many weeks, and affected an area that stretched from Spain and Italy in the south to the United Kingdom in the north throughout the month of August. Record temperatures were set in several countries, and at least 35,000 people died. Because it was not clear in many cases whether people died of heat-related illnesses, some experts put the total death toll as high as 52,000.

## Weather patterns

**Meteorologists** are not sure what caused the 2003 heat wave. Their studies revealed that the surface temperatures of the Atlantic Ocean (west of Europe) and the Mediterranean Sea (south of the continent) were higher than usual. In addition, the seasonal **monsoon** *(mahn SOON)* winds in West Africa were stronger and reached farther north than usual. Both these and other weather patterns may have played a part in causing the heat wave.

**Average daytime land surface temperatures in 2001 and 2003 are compared on a satellite image of Europe. Orange indicates where temperatures were up to 18 Fahrenheit (10 Celsius) degrees warmer in July 2003 compared with the same month in 2001. White areas show where temperatures were similar, and blue areas show where temperatures were cooler in 2003 than in 2001.**

People cool off in the fountains of London's Battersea Park during the European heat wave of 2003.

## Record temperatures

In 2003, the average temperature in Europe was 6.3 Fahrenheit (3.5 Celsius) degrees above normal. In some countries, temperatures broke all-time records. In the United Kingdom, the **thermometer** rose to 100.6 °F (38.1 °C) on August 10, the first 100 °F reading the country had experienced since record-keeping began in 1875. The record temperature for Switzerland went even higher—up to 106.7 °F (41.5 °C) on August 11. A record 104.7 °F (40.4 °C) was reached on August 13 in Germany, which also underwent a **drought.** Water levels on such large rivers as the Elbe and the Danube were so low that ships could not travel on them.

## HOW MANY DIED?

In October 2003, the Earth Policy Institute issued preliminary figures showing that more than 35,000 people had died from the heat during the summer of 2003. In 2006, the institute did follow-up research that indicated the true numbers of deaths may have been even higher.

| Country | Number of deaths |
|---|---|
| France | 14,802 |
| Germany | 7,000 |
| Spain | 4,230 |
| Italy | 4,175 |
| United Kingdom | 2,045 |
| Netherlands | 1,400 |
| Portugal | 1,316 |
| Belgium | 150 |
| **TOTAL** | **35,118** |

### In France

At the beginning of August 2003, temperatures in France soared to 104 °F (40 °C) and remained extremely high for two weeks. Such high temperatures were particularly unusual in northern France, where most people are used to mild summers. Few homes in France have **air conditioning,** which would have helped to keep people cool. In the countryside, farm animals died by the millions and crops withered in the heat. France's 2003 wheat harvest produced 20 percent less grain than usual, and by mid-August, winegrowers were harvesting grapes that would not normally be ready for picking until September.

By August 11, the situation was so bad that the French authorities began to worry about the safety of the country's 58 **nuclear power reactors,** which produce more than three-quarters of France's electric power. The temperature of some of the reactors came close to the safety limit of 122 °F (50 °C), despite their being sprayed with water to cool them down. Officials at some nuclear plants were given special permission to discharge very warm water into nearby rivers, which threatened fish and other animals.

French police patrol outside a refrigerated storage unit in Paris during the heat wave of 2003. The extreme heat resulted in so many deaths that authorities were forced to temporarily store bodies in food storage facilities.

## August vacations

Many French people traditionally take a long vacation during August, when some companies and stores close for the whole month. In 2003, this practice caused many people, including large numbers of doctors, nurses, and other hospital workers to be away from their jobs in the city during the worst of the heat wave. As a result, emergency cases could not be treated as quickly as usual. In addition, most hospitals had no air conditioning and quickly ran out of ice. The country's **morgues** *(MOHRGZ)* were overwhelmed as well. Eventually, authorities were forced to use refrigerated food storage facilities and to set up air-conditioned tents to handle the flood of dead bodies. Some government officials, including the health minister, were also away on vacation. They were later criticized for not returning to their offices to introduce emergency measures.

**An elderly woman suffering from the effects of heat holds a damp towel over her head as she is brought by firefighters to a hospital in Paris during the heat wave of 2003.**

### ELDERLY PEOPLE

As is usually the case with heat waves, older people, who could not withstand the effects of **heat stroke** and **dehydration,** suffered the most. More than 65 percent of the nearly 15,000 deaths in France were in the over-75 age group. While many of the heat-wave victims died in hospitals and retirement homes, some died at home alone because their families were away on vacation. Many bodies were not claimed for weeks because relatives were away.

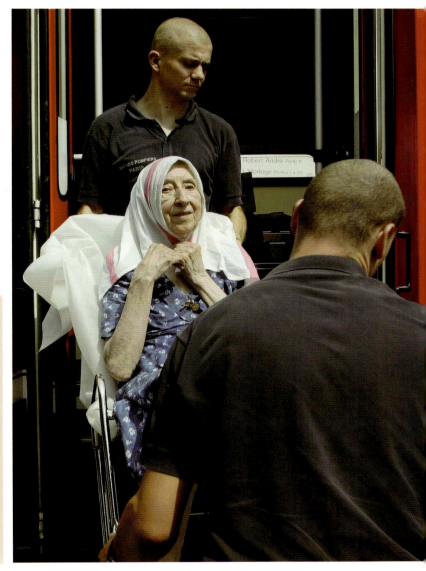

# STUDYING HEAT WAVES

Scientists have studied heat—and heat waves—for hundreds of years. **Meteorologists** study weather. **Climatologists** study **climate,** which is the kind of weather a place has over a period of years. Climate includes conditions of heat and cold. In 1593, Italian astronomer and physicist Galileo (1564–1642) developed a **thermometer** that used water to indicate air temperature. By the 1800's, scientists were using weather maps to forecast the weather.

**A Stevenson screen, containing thermometers and other meteorological measuring and recording devices, is designed to protect the devices while allowing the free movement of air around them.**

Today, scientists use sensitive instruments to measure temperature changes all over the world. They can input the results into powerful computers and compare the statistics over long periods. They can also create computer models, which can *simulate* (represent) how **weather systems** form and change. These can include heat waves. Scientists hope that by studying the statistics and models, they will be able to predict future climate changes.

## Learning from the past

Scientists can study past climates by looking at such natural sources as tree rings or ice cores. Scientists take tree samples by driving a metal tube into an ancient tree. This tube retrieves a core of wood from the outer bark to the center of the trunk. Experts can then examine the sample, which shows a growth ring for every year. The width of each ring is affected by temperature, rainfall, and other weather factors during the year in which it formed. In the same way, tubes can be driven into ice sheets to obtain core samples. Experts analyze air and other substances in the ice to get information on past climate.

**Paleoclimatologists** (PAY lee oh kly muh TAH luh jists)—scientists who study the climate of prehistoric times—have learned that Earth's temperature has gone up and down over hundreds, thousands, and millions of years. They have found that there was a long period of hotter weather about 55 million years ago, long before human beings walked on Earth.

### GABRIEL DANIEL FAHRENHEIT

Gabriel Daniel Fahrenheit (1686–1736), a German physicist, found a way to measure temperature accurately. He invented a thermometer that used mercury inside a very thin, sealed glass tube that was partially filled with liquid. This kind of thermometer is still used today. Fahrenheit also developed the temperature scale that is named for him. He used 32 °F (0 °C) for the freezing point of water and 212 °F (100 °C) for the boiling point of water.

Scientists in Antarctica set up a lightweight drilling system to extract ice core samples from deep within the Antarctic ice sheet. Data from these samples provide evidence of past changes in climate.

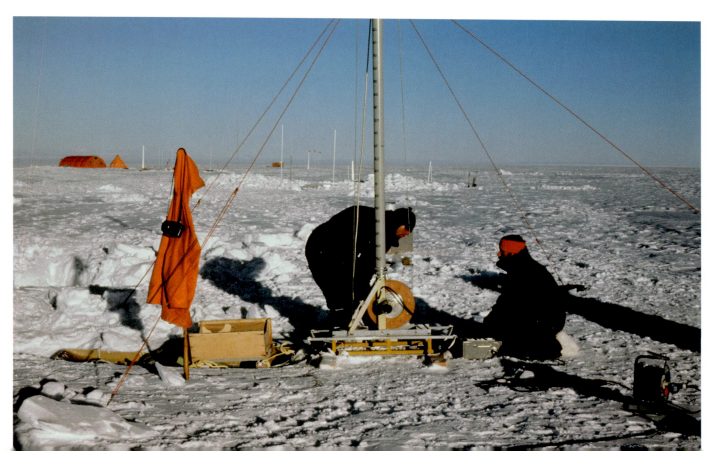

# HEAT ISLANDS

If you watch a local weather forecast on television, you may notice that temperatures are often higher in the cities than *rural* (country) areas. In fact, cities may be up to 10 Fahrenheit (5.6 Celsius) degrees warmer than the surrounding countryside. The city is normally warmest at the center and forms a circular or oval-shaped "urban **heat island**" in the green "ocean" that surrounds it. On the urban island itself, parks, open land, lakes, and ponds create cooler areas. The bigger the urban area, the larger the heat island. If there is a heat wave, the island, naturally, will be even hotter than the rest of the region.

**The heat island profile of a typical city shows that temperatures are highest in dense downtown areas and lowest in parks and rural areas.**

**Urban heat island profile**

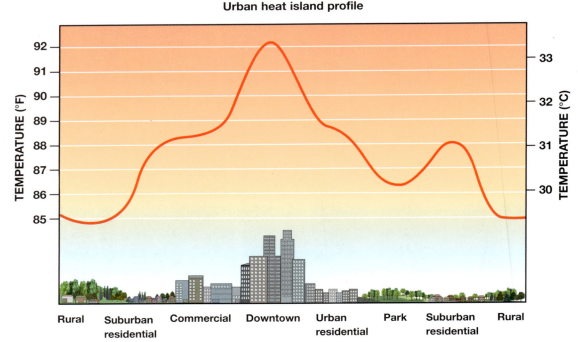

Source: U.S. Environmental Protection Agency.

## How do they form?

Heat islands form for a number of reasons. Concrete, asphalt, tar, brick, and stone do not reflect the sun well but soak up its heat. They can store this heat for long periods, which makes buildings hotter than open land. Tall buildings and narrow streets heat the air that is trapped between them. Waste gases and particles from factories, cars, and **air-conditioning** units contain a great deal of heat and contribute to the formation of a blanket of **pollution** that does not allow the heat to escape. Trees and plants, which provide shade and give off water vapor from their leaves, have a natural cooling effect in parks and the countryside.

## At night

The building materials found in cities tend to retain the heat at night, when the air temperature cools. Because of this quality, the biggest temperature difference between urban and rural areas—or maximum heat island effect—usually occurs three to five hours after sunset. The effects of a heat wave are often felt more strongly in urban areas because the temperature drops less at night. A study in Barcelona, Spain, found that the city's nighttime temperature was generally 5.2 Fahrenheit (2.9 Celsius) degrees warmer than that of the surrounding countryside.

A thermometer reads 50 °C (122 °F) in central Seville, Spain, during a heat wave in June 2004. The effects of a heat wave are worse in the city because of the heat island effect.

## LOS ANGELES

On July 17, 1955, a heat wave in Los Angeles made conditions uncomfortable for visitors on the opening day of the Disneyland theme park in nearby Anaheim. Few water fountains had been installed because of a plumbers' strike, and ladies' high heels kept getting stuck in the asphalt roads, which had been poured the night before. By the following month, the heat had increased. An eight-day period of temperatures above 100 °F (37.8 °C) caused 946 deaths in the city. The **thermometer** reached 110 °F (43.3 °C), compared with the normal average August temperature of 71 °F (21.7 °C).

A heat wave hit Chicago for a week beginning on July 11, 1995. It was not the first heat wave to strike the city, which acts as an urban **heat island,** but it caused the greatest number of deaths. The official total was 521 heat-related deaths during the month of July, with 465 deaths occurring during the heat-wave week. Later, records showed that 739 more Chicagoans had died that month than the usual number for July. Many medical examiners believe that such a comparison is a more accurate measure of heat-related deaths. The number of deaths was so high that the city's **morgues** did not have room to store all the bodies. Refrigerated trucks were brought in to hold the bodies until they could be examined and identified. The remains of at least 170 people never claimed by family members were later buried in mass graves.

**Public health workers wheel bodies into refrigerated trucks during the Chicago heat wave of 1995. With hundreds of people dying from the heat, the city's morgues were overwhelmed.**

## Highs and lows

The average temperature for Chicago in July is 73 °F (22.8 °C), which was the exact temperature on Monday, July 3. Just eight days later, 73 °F was the nighttime low. During the day, the temperature rose to 90 °F (32.2 °C). The following day, the *Chicago Sun-Times* newspaper featured an article entitled "Heat Wave on the Way—And It Can Be a Killer." By Thursday, July 13, the temperature was up to 106 °F (41.1 °C), a record high for Chicago in July. But it felt even

A man and his son pray at a mass grave in August 1995, where more than 40 of the unclaimed victims of Chicago's heat wave await burial.

hotter to the people of the city because the **heat index** rose to 125 °F (52 °C), which is in the "extreme danger" zone.

## Sweltering at home

During heat waves in the 1930's, many Chicagoans left their apartments or houses to sleep in the open air in one of the city's parks or along the shore of Lake Michigan where it was cooler. But crime rates were much higher in 1995 than in the 1930's. As a result, many residents, especially older people, did not want to leave their homes or even open their windows or doors to let in slightly cooler air because they were afraid that they might be robbed or attacked.

### EIGHTY YEARS EARLIER

In 1915, a heat wave in Chicago caused 535 deaths. The next year's Cook County Hospital *Annual Report* described the scene: "… our employees worked day and night almost without sleep trying to save the lives of over 200 persons who were overcome by heat. The patients were not merely given a bath and put to bed. They had to be put in large bath tubs filled with ice water and rubbed for half an hour or more until their temperatures were brought somewhere near normal. When they were brought into the hospital, their temperatures could not be registered, for they were higher than the **thermometer** would record, 110 degrees [F] [43.3 °C]."

## Emergency problems

City officials were slow to warn the people of Chicago about the dangers of the heat wave. The city's roads buckled and railway lines warped from the heat, causing long delays for people going to work and for freight being moved through Chicago's large network of tracks. Children traveling to summer school in school buses became so overheated and **dehydrated** that they had to be hosed down by fire fighters. People opened more than 3,000 hydrants in the streets, which caused whole neighborhoods to lose water pressure. At the same time, the use of **air conditioners** (by those who had them) led to power failures. At one point, 49,000 households were without electric power. By Friday, July 14, the city's emergency services could not keep up with the number of calls, and 23 hospitals had to close their emergency rooms. Ambulance crews were forced to drive around the city looking for a health facility for their patients.

**The stress of working in extreme temperatures shows on the face of an exhausted police officer during the Chicago heat wave of 1995.**

## Old and alone

Most of the heat-wave victims were poor, elderly people living in the city. Most either had no air-conditioning or could not afford to turn it on. About 50 percent of the people who died were over the age of 75; another 25 percent were between 65 and 75. Many of the victims lived alone and died without ever requesting medical help.

## Learning from mistakes

City officials did not issue an emergency warning until the last day of the heat wave. Chicago had five special cooling centers—air-conditioned buildings where water and sometimes medical attention were provided—but they were not fully used. Eventually, the mayor of Chicago set up an emergency heat command center. Instructions were broadcast advising people on how to "beat the heat." Some of these measures were useful just two weeks later, when hot weather returned to Chicago. The second heat wave, however, was shorter and less severe.

### FOUR YEARS LATER

Chicago had another serious heat wave in 1999, and the city put its Extreme Weather Operations Plan into effect immediately. The authorities issued warnings and phoned elderly people. They also opened 34 cooling centers and sent officers door to door to check on people who lived alone. The result of these efforts was that there were 103 heat-related deaths, less than one-sixth the number who died in 1995.

**A nurse checks on a man at one of the cooling centers set up in Chicago during the second heat wave to hit the city in July 1995.**

# HEAT WAVE OF 1936

In the summer of 1936, the people of the United States struggled through a fifth year of a devastating drought that created fierce **dust storms.** At the same time, the worst heat wave in U.S. history brought additional misery to much of the country. In some areas, temperatures climbed to 120 °F (48.9 °C). The 1936 heat wave claimed at least 5,000 lives.

## Dust Bowl

A severe drought struck the southern Great Plains of the United States from 1931 to 1938. It began when average rainfall dropped by about 35 percent. The soil dried out, and crops began to fail. At the same time, the region was blasted by periodic heat waves. Prairie grasses died, and as natural vegetation and such crops as wheat disappeared, the soil was left bare. Soon huge dust storms started to blow. These storms caused one of the worst environmental disasters in U.S. history. The drought region came to be known as the Dust Bowl. Altogether, the heat and drought damaged about 50 million acres (20 million hectares), mainly in Colorado, Kansas, New Mexico, Oklahoma, and Texas.

## Record temperatures

The most severe Dust Bowl heat wave began in late June 1936 and continued into July. Temperatures climbed to over 100 °F (37.8 °C) across two-thirds of the United States. An area of high pressure moved north, bringing high temperatures with it. By August, new temperature records had been set in 16 states.

Rex Tugwell, a close advisor to U.S. President Franklin Delano Roosevelt, examines dust and sand that covers what had been a prosperous farm near Dalhart, Texas, in August 1936. Dust storms, caused by heat waves and years of drought, damaged thousands of acres of farmland on the southern Great Plains, a region then called the Dust Bowl.

The heat moved up to Canada, where temperatures reached new heights—111 °F (43.9 °C) in Manitoba and 108 °F (42.2 °C) in Ontario. By the time it was over, this devastating heat wave had caused nearly 5,000 deaths in the United States and nearly 800 in Canada. Another 400 Canadians were indirect victims of the heat wave, including people who drowned while trying to stay cool.

**Grasshoppers swarm over a window screen in a South Dakota farmhouse during the summer of 1936. Compounding the problems of heat and drought, a plague of grasshoppers devoured farmers' already withered crops across the Great Plains and as far north as Minnesota and the Dakotas.**

## Temperature records set in 1936

| State | Location | Date | °F (°C) |
|-------|----------|------|---------|
| Arkansas | Ozark | Aug. 10 | 120* (48.9*) |
| Indiana | Collegeville | July 14 | 116* (46.7*) |
| Kansas | Alton | July 24 | 121* (49.4*) |
| Louisiana | Plain Dealing | Aug. 10 | 114* (45.6*) |
| Maryland | Cumberland | July 10 | 109* (42.8*) |
| Michigan | Mio | July 13 | 112* (44.4*) |
| Minnesota | Moorhead | July 6 | 114* (45.6*) |
| Nebraska | Minden | July 24 | 118* (47.8*) |
| New Jersey | Runyon | July 10 | 110* (43.3*) |
| North Dakota | Steele | July 6 | 121* (49.4*) |
| Oklahoma | Alva | July 18 | 120 (48.9) |
| Pennsylvania | Phoenixville | July 10 | 111* (43.9*) |
| South Dakota | Gann Valley | July 5 | 120* (48.9*) |
| Texas | Seymour | Aug. 12 | 120 (48.9) |
| West Virginia | Martinsburg | July 10 | 112* (44.4*) |
| Wisconsin | Wisconsin Dells | July 13 | 114* (45.6*) |

*Still the state record in 2007.          Source: U.S. National Oceanic and Atmospheric Administration.

## WITHERED CROPS

An account of the heat wave in *Newsweek* magazine reported:

"Withering heat, rushing out of the furnace of the prairie dust bowl, blasted crops, sucked up rivers and lakes, and transformed the nation—from the Rockies to the Atlantic—into a vast simmering cauldron. By the end of last week, two-thirds of the United States broiled under a lethal sky. Temperatures climbed to 120 degrees. In the Dakotas, Minnesota, Montana, and Wyoming, farmers stumbled into dusty fields to gaze helplessly at dying wheat. Other grains charred. On seared pastures gaunt livestock sickened."

As the Plains baked, the heat wave rolled across Illinois, Indiana, and Michigan, and then across West Virginia and Pennsylvania into New York and New Jersey. In New York City, thousands of people were trapped in Manhattan as the heat warped the metal joints on moveable bridges across the East and Harlem rivers, locking them in an upright position. Athletes competing for a slot on the U.S. Olympic team collapsed in the heat.

To escape the oppressive heat, many residents of Detroit slept out in the open on Belle Isle, an island park in the Detroit River, during the 1936 heat wave.

### Disaster in Detroit

In 1936, Detroit, Michigan, had recorded only seven days of 100 °F (37.8 °C) readings in more than 60 years of official weather record keeping. Beginning on July 8, however, temperatures topped 100 °F for seven straight days, including two days with **thermometers** registering over 104 °F (40 °C). **Air-conditioned** movie theatres—among the few places with temperature control—put up signs saying, "It's cool inside." Heat-wave victims found little relief in sweltering hospitals, where the oppressive heat and humidity claimed doctors and nurses as well. Hundreds of thousands of families fled to nearby Belle Isle, an island park in the Detroit River, to sleep in the open. Detroit's heat wave, which ended in a huge afternoon thunderstorm on July 14, killed at least 364 people in the city.

## News account

A July 1936 issue of *Newsweek* magazine described the suffering in Detroit: "Hospital corridors in Detroit were filled with screaming victims and relatives as the fatal sun rose higher. Weeping crowds attempted to force their way into the morgue, where emergency slabs cared for bodies arriving in a steady stream. Sheets ran out, and dead lay uncovered while police sirens signalled new arrivals. More than 100 heat casualties occurred in 24 hours."

### THE PENNY FUND

In 1938, as heat waves continued, the *Detroit News* and Salvation Army set up the Penny Fund, selling blocks of ice for a penny each. The purpose of the charge was to avoid making people feel that they were accepting charity. The availability of ice significantly reduced the death rate among the chief victims of heat waves—infants, the elderly, and the sick.

**People collect ice from a Salvation Army truck during a 1938 heat wave in Detroit. They paid a penny for up to 50 pounds (23 kilograms) of ice.**

# AUSTRALIA, 1923–1924

Most of Australia has a hot, dry climate. The northern third lies in the **tropics,** and so is warm all year round. In this region, there are two seasons—a wet season and a dry one. The wet season corresponds with summer and lasts from November through April. In many places away from the northern coast, however, there is very little rain at any time of the year. Much of the country is covered by dry **desert.** Because of its climate, Australia often undergoes severe heat waves. In 1896, 437 people died of heat-related causes. During the 1900's, heat waves caused more deaths in Australia than any other natural hazard. One of the worst heat waves took place in 1923–1924.

## Longest heat wave

A sign in Marble Bar, Australia, claims that the town is the country's "hottest spot."

The small town of Marble Bar, Western Australia, 114 miles (184 kilometers) southeast of Port Headland on the Indian Ocean coast, lies at the edge of the Great Sandy Desert. It is said to be the hottest town in Australia, with temperatures higher than 100 °F (37.8 °C) on more

than 150 days each year and a record high of 120.5 °F (49.2 °C). The town also holds the record for the longest number of days in a row with temperatures above 100 °F. The record was set from Oct. 31,1923, to April 7, 1924—a total of 160 days, or more than 5 months. The highest temperature—117.5 °F (47.5 °C)—was reached on January 18, at the height of the Australian summer.

## No lows

Just as heat waves are generally created by areas of high **air pressure,** they often end when a low pressure weather system comes along. In the northwest Australian region, lows sometimes move in from the Indian Ocean with **monsoon** winds or **tropical cyclones.** Both of these wind systems bring rain. But in 1923–1924, there were no monsoons or cyclones in the region. In fact, there were just two, short rainstorms in the Marble Bar area during the whole heat wave period.

### DESERTS

The Great Sandy Desert is one of four major deserts that together cover about one-third of Australia. The Great Sandy, Great Victoria, and Simpson deserts are made up of rock, scrub, and sand. The surface of the Gibson Desert consists mainly of small stones and pebbles. All sandy or rocky deserts are hot during the day. The highest temperature ever recorded—136 °F (58 °C)—occurred in Libya, at the northern edge of the world's largest desert, the Sahara.

**Maximum temperatures at Marble Bar over the period Oct. 31, 1923, to April 7, 1924. The highest temperature recorded at the peak of the heat wave was 117.5 °F (47.5 °C) on Jan. 18.**

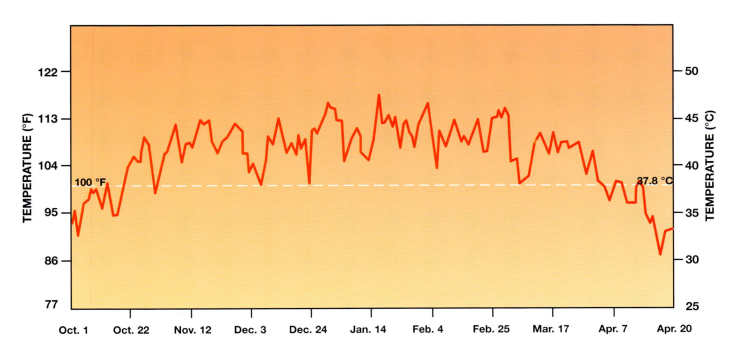

# HUMAN INFLUENCE

Researchers in the United Kingdom who studied the 2003 European heat wave concluded that human activities were at least partly to blame for the extreme temperatures. Most scientists have also concluded that human activities have played a significant role in the general effect of **global warming,** an increase in the average temperature of Earth's surface. Since the late 1800's, the global average temperature has increased by 0.7 to 1.4 Fahrenheit (0.4 to 0.8 Celsius) degrees. Many experts have estimated that the average temperature will rise an additional 2.5 to 10.4 Fahrenheit (1.4 to 5.8 Celsius) degrees by 2100.

## More heat waves?

**Cars pass a sign giving information about water restrictions on the outskirts of Goulburn in Australia during a 10-year drought that continued in 2007.**

The authors of a 2004 study conducted by U.S. researchers estimated that heat waves in some parts of the world would become more severe in the 2000's. They may also occur more often and last longer. Following the heat waves of 1995 in Chicago and 2003 in Paris, the scientists concentrated their research on those two cities. They predicted that the average number of heat waves would increase

during the 2000's by 25 percent in Chicago and nearly 33 percent in Paris. In both cities, the scientists said, a typical heat wave could last up to four days longer.

## Greenhouse effect

Most scientists believe that human activities contribute to global warming by adding to the natural **greenhouse effect** of Earth's **atmosphere.** Earth's atmosphere acts like the glass of a greenhouse, trapping air that is heated by the sun. The gases that trap heat in the atmosphere are known as **greenhouse gases.** The main human activities that increase the amount of greenhouse gases involve burning **fossil fuels,** such as coal, oil, and natural gas, and clearing land for farming by burning trees. Fossil fuels are burned to provide power for cars, factories, and power plants that generate electric power for houses and office buildings.

### GLOBAL IMPACTS

Many scientists believe that global warming could cause more extreme weather. In the future, human beings may experience more—and more severe—heat waves, **droughts, floods,** and damaging storms, such as **hurricanes.** Global warming could cause polar ice to melt, raising the sea level along the coasts in certain parts of the world. Tropical diseases, such as **malaria,** might spread to larger regions. Crop yields could decline. The warming effect might harm plants and animals that live in the sea. It could also force animals and plants on land to move to new **habitats.**

**Emissions pour from a power plant on the outskirts of Beijing, China. Many scientists believe that the burning of fossil fuels in such plants is contributing to the levels of greenhouse gases in Earth's atmosphere.**

# DROUGHTS AND FIRES

Heat waves are often accompanied by **droughts**—long periods of dry weather—and can cause **wildfires.** Because of this connection, we tend to think of droughts as hot, dry spells. The shortage of water has a great impact on plants, animals, and people.

Wildfires are one of the most devastating results of drought. When plants have withered and dried out, they act as **tinder** for the slightest spark. Once a blaze starts, it can spread rapidly through dry litter lying on the forest floor or across dried-out grassland.

## Black Friday

In the summer of 1938–1939, southern Australia experienced a combination of heat and drought that turned very deadly. During the first week of January 1939, a high-pressure system stalled over the southern coast, and very hot air moved in from the central deserts of Australia. A severe heat wave started on January 6 and lasted for a week. The highest temperature— 114 °F (45.6 °C)—was reached on Friday, January 13. By that time, there had been so little rain since spring that most of the vegetation in the region had dried out.

On January 13, a day that came to be known as Black Friday, millions of acres of mountain-ash forest and scrub were set alight as strong, hot winds drove several smaller fires

**The remains of a forest after the disastrous fires that destroyed large areas of the Australian state of Victoria in 1939.**

together. Several towns were destroyed, and 50 people died. Altogether, three-quarters of the state of Victoria was affected by the disaster. Later, the Royal Commission reported: "It appeared the whole State was alight on Friday, 13 January, 1939." During the month of January, 438 people died of heat-related causes in the three states of New South Wales, South Australia, and Victoria.

**A girl wades in shallow waters as a helicopter refills its water tank to fight wildfires on the hills beyond the lake as wildfires again threatened the Australian state of Victoria in 2006 during a prolonged drought and heat wave.**

## PROLONGED DROUGHT IN AUSTRALIA

In the early 2000's, Australia experienced its worst drought in at least a century. By 2007, some areas of Australia had been under drought conditions for 10 years. The state premier of Queensland, Peter Beattie, announced in January that the situation was so dire that unless conditions changed, people in the state would be forced to drink recycled sewage water in 2008. In March 2007, experts reported that the country's 1 million *feral* (wild) camels were being driven mad by thirst. The animals were reported to have trampled fences, tanks and pipes in their frantic search for water. Wildfires in December 2006 in southeastern Australia burned more than 445,000 acres (180,000 acres) across four states.

# UNITED STATES, 1980'S

A number of heat waves devastated parts of the United States throughout the 1980's. Record temperatures and **droughts** were recorded in 1980, 1983, 1986, 1988, and 1989. In the disastrous heat wave of 1980, which struck the central and eastern parts of the United States, deaths from heat stress were estimated at 10,000. At least 5,000 people—and possibly twice that number—died from heat-related illness in the same region in 1988.

**A South Carolina farmer displays ears of corn severely stunted by the 1986 heat wave and drought, which devastated crops in the southern United States.**

## 1980

The 1980 heat wave began in June when an area of high pressure sent temperatures soaring above 90 °F (32.2 °C) in the central part of the country. Temperatures remained stuck at that level almost daily for the next four months. In Kansas City, Missouri, the temperature stayed above the 100 °F (37.8 °C) mark for more than two weeks and in Dallas and Fort Worth, Texas, for 42 consecutive days. Altogether, 26 states were affected by the heat wave.

## Damage to agriculture

The 1980 heat wave caused property losses of about $20 billion. Farmers experienced the greatest losses as high temperatures damaged crops and caused the deaths of thousands of farm animals. Corn and soybean harvests were particularly affected. Spring wheat, which is planted in the spring and becomes fully ripe in summer, also suffered. (Winter wheat, which is planted in the autumn and harvested in late spring and early summer, was harvested before the worst of the heat wave set in.) Livestock suffered, as grazing grasses were destroyed in the Great Plains states. An estimated 5 million chickens, which cannot tolerate temperatures much above 80 °F (27 °C), died during the heat wave of 1980.

**A Texas rancher reaches down as far as his elbow into a crack in the bottom of a dry stock pond in search of any sign of moisture during the prolonged drought and heat wave in 1980.**

## CELSIUS SCALE

People in all major countries of the world except the United States use the Celsius scale for everyday temperature measurement. Scientists also use this metric scale (sometimes called centigrade), which was developed in 1742 by Swedish astronomer Anders Celsius (1701-1744). It was later changed and improved. The ninth General Conference of Weights and Measures officially named it the Celsius scale in 1948. On the Celsius scale, 0° is the freezing point of water, and 100° is the boiling point.

## Windstorms

During the 1980 heat wave, several severe windstorms called **derechos** *(deh-RAY-chos)* hit the United States. A derecho is a widespread and long-lived windstorm that is usually associated with a band of rapidly moving showers or thunderstorms. The winds in a derecho (which means *straight ahead* in Spanish) usually blow in one direction. These storms may be hundreds of miles long. On July 4 and 5, 1980, a derecho raced from eastern Nebraska to Virginia, with gusts blowing at more than 80 miles (128 kilometers) per hour. The storm became known as the "More Trees Down" derecho because so many were blown down. Six people were killed and 67 others were injured by the derecho winds. Ten days later, another derecho caused property damage in Wisconsin.

## Throughout the 1980's

A severe heat wave and **drought** hit parts of the southeastern United States in the summer of 1986, causing about 100 deaths. The situation was much worse two years later in the central and eastern areas of the country. In 1988, soaring temperatures caused up to 10,000 heat-related deaths and property losses of about $40 billion. The highest temperatures occurred in June, when 69 cities registered record setting temperatures for the month.

### SUMMER 2006

In 2006, at least 225 people died from the severe heat in July and August. California was especially hard hit. Sacramento, the capital, suffered through 11 consecutive days of temperatures exceeding 100 °F (37.8 °C). In Los Angeles County, the temperature reached 119 °F (48.3 °C). Officials said the heat wave was the worst to hit both the northern and southern parts of the state at the same time in 57 years. The 2006 California heat wave killed more than 25,000 heads of cattle and 800,000 poultry.

## Energy problems

The heat wave of 1988 caused major problems with energy supplies. Utility companies could not produce enough electric power, as **air-conditioning** units hummed continually. Electric-power companies could generate only an additional 2 percent of power as demand rose by 6 percent. The gap resulted partly from drought-related low water levels in rivers which limited the output of **hydroelectric** dams. In addition, some **nuclear power** plants had to cut their output because of a lack of water for the units' cooling systems.

**Dairy cows at a farm in California are showered with water to keep them cool during the heat wave of 2006, which killed more than 25,000 head of cattle.**

# CARING FOR ANIMALS

Heat waves can be as dangerous for animals as they are for people. They can be especially challenging for livestock farmers, whose animals must have plenty of shade and water. Shortages of drinking water during heat waves can aggravate the problem.

**Pet dogs cool down in a park fountain in Taipei, Taiwan, as a heat wave scorches the island in August 2003.**

## Helping pets

Here are some important ways to help keep pets safe during very hot weather:

- Never leave an animal in a car. On hot days, cars heat up quickly and can reach more than 140 °F (60 °C) in minutes, even if you leave the windows open. Mobile homes also heat up quickly.

- Don't let your pet get sunburned. Animals with a naturally thin coat of fur or whose fur has been trimmed close to their skin can get sunburn. Owners should cover any exposed area, especially ear tips, with sunblock before the animal goes outside.

- Make sure all pets can find shade and have a constant supply of fresh, cool drinking water.

■ Giving animals a cool bath or shower will help keep their body temperature down. A damp towel on a tile floor or a damp towel or washcloth over the skin will also help cool the animal.

■ All cages and enclosures should be kept in the shade. Watch out for warning signs of **heat stroke,** including rapid panting, wide eyes, drooling, hot skin, twitching muscles, vomiting, or a dazed look. If in doubt, contact a veterinarian for advice.

■ Don't exercise dogs in the heat. During hot weather, walk your dog early in the morning or late in the evening, when it will not burn its paws on the hot ground or be at increased risk of heat stroke.

■ Keep indoor fish tanks out of direct sunlight. Change the water regularly and keep it clear of algae. Frequently top off water levels in fishponds to replace liquid lost to evaporation and to increase levels of dissolved oxygen, which fall during hot weather.

## KEEPING COOL!

Zoo animals must be kept cool during heat waves, too. Handlers use all sorts of different methods to help the animals. In summer 2006, the weather was so hot in Zurich, Switzerland, that handlers started freezing food in blocks of ice before giving it to the animals. The animals were kept cool as they licked and chewed their way through the ice toward their food.

**Baribal bears are fed mackerel-flavored ice blocks to keep them cool at a zoo outside Paris during the European heat wave of 2003.**

# HEAT WAVE WARNINGS

The United States National Weather Service issues warnings and advisories to alert the public about the dangers of extremely hot and humid weather. These warnings are based on the **heat index** (HI), a measure of how hot the air feels. The HI is measured in Fahrenheit degrees but takes into account the effects of both temperature and **relative humidity.** For example, if the temperature is 88 °F (31.1 °C) and the humidity is 80 percent, conditions are in the danger zone. Heat index values are based on air temperature in the shade with a light wind blowing. Exposure to direct sunlight or strong winds can significantly increase the HI.

## Heat-related danger

The higher the HI, the greater is the likelihood that people will develop heat-related illnesses. The index describes four levels of

**People seek respite from soaring temperatures in a swimming pool at Toshimaen Water Park in Tokyo, Japan, during a heat wave in 2005.**

danger for older people, people with certain medical conditions, and others in higher risk groups: caution, extreme caution, danger, and extreme danger.

- At the caution level (an HI value of 80 to 90 °F [27 to 32 °C]), susceptible people may suffer fatigue with prolonged exposure and/or physical activity.

- At the extreme caution level (90 to 105 °F [32 to 41 °C]), people may suffer sunstroke, **heat cramps,** or **heat exhaustion** with prolonged exposure and/or physical activity.

- At the danger level (105 to 130 °F [41 to 54 °C]), sunstroke, heat cramps, or heat exhaustion are likely and heat stroke is possible with prolonged exposure and/or physical activity.

- At the extreme danger level (130 °F [54 °C] or higher), heat stroke/sunstroke is highly likely with continued exposure.

## Heat warnings

The National Weather Service may issue an excessive heat advisory, watch, or warning, depending on the HI.

- An excessive heat advisory indicates that the HI is expected to reach at least 100 °F (38 °C) but less than 115 °F (46 °C) for less than three hours per day; nighttime lows are expected to remain above 80 °F (27 °C) for two consecutive days.

- An excessive heat watch indicates that it is possible that the HI will exceed 115 °F (46 °C) for any length of time or 105 °F (41 °C) for three or more hours for at least two consecutive days.

- An excessive heat warning indicates that the HI is expected to exceed 115 °F (46 °C) for any length of time or 105 °F (41 °C) for three or more hours for at least two consecutive days.

### HEAT/HEALTH WATCH WARNING SYSTEM

In 1993, the National Weather Service began implementing a special heat warning system for major U.S. cities based on local weather conditions, population, and the **heat island** effect there. By 2007, at least 16 cities had adopted the system. In general, the HI needed to trigger a warning in these cities is lower than that for smaller cities, towns, or rural areas.

# WEATHERING A HEAT WAVE

Emergency preparedness officials and public health experts offer the following guidelines for avoiding health problems during a heat wave.

## Food and drink

During a heat wave, drink plenty of fluids, even if you don't feel thirsty. It's important to drink regularly because your body needs water to keep cool and prevent **dehydration.** Experts advise adults to avoid drinks containing alcohol or caffeine because they dehydrate your body. You should also avoid large, heavy meals, especially those high in protein, because the body pumps out more heat to aid in digestion.

## Clothing

On very hot days, wear lightweight, light-colored clothes. Light colors reflect the sun's rays more than dark colors, which absorb the sun's heat. Loose-fitting clothes that cover as much skin as possible are best. Cotton is ideal for hot conditions because it lets air pass through, allowing sweat to **evaporate.** You should protect your face and head as much as possible by wearing a wide-brimmed hat.

A woman carries hand fans to sell in Kolkata, India, in 2003. Waving a hand fan creates an airflow that helps to increase heat loss and make the body more comfortable.

## Treating illness

Heat-related illnesses range from mild **heat exhaustion** to severe **heat stroke.** If a person is promptly treated for heat exhaustion, he or she can recover without any lasting problems. Someone with symptoms of heat exhaustion needs to be cooled quickly. Symptoms include faintness, headache, and nausea. The skin may become cold, gray, and moist with sweat. In most cases, body temperature remains about normal. Get the person to take a cool shower or bath or use a spray bottle to mist the person and his or her clothes. Fan the person to increase heat loss.

Heat stroke is a severe medical emergency because the body's cooling mechanisms are completely overwhelmed. Body temperature may climb to 105 °F (41 °C). Heat stroke can lead to brain damage or failure of the kidneys or **cardiovascular system.** If you suspect that a person is suffering from heat stroke, you should call emergency services immediately. Spray the person with water or wrap in cool, wet towels or sheets until emergency help arrives. Repeated dips in cool water may also help cool the body. Heat-stroke victims should slowly drink a half glass of cool water every 15 minutes, unless they are vomiting or are not fully conscious.

**People suffering from heat stroke receive intravenous treatment at a hospital in Xi'an, China, during a heat wave in 2004.**

## HEAT CRAMPS

**Heat cramps** are painful muscle spasms that are caused by excessive sweating, which leads to a loss of salt. This condition is not as serious as heat exhaustion or heat stroke. Anyone suffering from heat cramps should be moved as quickly as possible to a cooler place, where he or she can rest in a comfortable position. Cool water should be drunk regularly—about half a glass every 15 minutes. The affected muscles can be lightly stretched.

Scientists have learned a great deal about heat waves—what they are, how they happen, and the effects they have. This knowledge is useful for public officials planning for or managing the effects of a heat wave and for people attempting to avoid heat-related illnesses.

## Air conditioning

Surveys of heat wave disasters in the United States and elsewhere have shown that **air conditioning** saves lives. According to the National Disaster Education Coalition in Washington, D.C., spending at least two hours a day in air conditioning during a heat wave significantly lowers a person's risk of heat-related illness. Because many people do not have air conditioning at home, cities often provide cooling centers and other public facilities.

The problem with air-conditioning units is that they use a great deal of energy. In the past, their use has caused power shortages during long heat waves. **Environmentalists** and others are also concerned that air conditioning contributes to the emission of **greenhouse gases** and may add to the problems of **global warming** (see pages 28-29).

**New Yorkers cross the Brooklyn Bridge from Manhattan during an electrical power outage caused by hot weather. Affecting large parts of northeastern North America, on Aug. 14, 2003, the power outage shut down New York's subway system.**

## Cool and green roofs

A *cool roof* reflects the sun well, keeping the inside of the building cool. It is light colored and can be particularly effective on buildings with a large roof area. In Chicago, the city's energy code requires that roof installations on commercial, air-conditioned buildings be highly reflective to help reduce the urban **heat island** effect. Another alternative is a green roof, which is planted with vegetation. The roof has a layer of soil that can support grass and other plants. On hot days, the surface of a green roof may be cooler than the surrounding air, while an ordinary dark roof may be 90 Fahrenheit (50 Celsius) degrees hotter than the air.

### ROOFTOP GARDENS

After the heat waves of 1995, urban planners in Chicago searched for additional ways to lower city temperatures naturally during the summer. One of these is the green roof program. In 2000, the city planted a 20,300-square-foot (1,886-square-meter) garden on the roof of City Hall. The garden helps to reduce the urban heat island effect. It also absorbs much of the rain that falls on the building, lowering the amount of runoff that sewers must manage during a storm.

The 10.4-acre (4.2 hectare) "living roof" on the Ford Motor Company Rouge Center in Dearborn, Michigan, is planted with sedum, a drought-resistant groundcover.

## MAKE YOUR OWN THERMOMETER

A **thermometer** is an instrument for measuring temperature. You can make your own simple version.

### Equipment

- Clear, narrow-necked glass or plastic bottle about 6 inches (15 centimeters) tall (the narrower the better)
- Lukewarm water (quantity depending on size of bottle)
- Clear plastic drinking straw
- Index card, ruler, bowl, tape
- Modeling clay
- Food coloring
- Thermometer

### Instructions

**1.** Pour the water into the bottle so that it is about a quarter full. Add a few drops of food coloring and mix.

**2.** Mold modeling clay around the straw, about 1.5 inches (4 centimeters) from the end. Put the straw in the bottle, but don't let it touch the bottom. Mold the clay around the bottle neck to keep the straw in place and make the bottle airtight.

**3.** Leave the bottle for an hour at room temperature. Attach an index card to the bottle with tape. Note the level of the water and mark a line showing the level on the card. Use a real thermometer to check the temperature of the room, and write the figure next to your line.

**4.** Put the bottle in a bowl of very warm water. The colored water in the straw will rise. When it has stopped rising, mark the level on the index card with a line. Write the real temperature next to the second line and see how it differs from your first temperature reading. You may want to keep a record book, checking temperatures at different times of day (early morning, noon, evening), in different places (sunny windowsill, basement), or over a week or longer.

—72 °F (22 °C)

**air conditioning** A system that controls temperature and humidity in a building or vehicle.

**air mass** A large body of air at a particular temperature, humidity, and height.

**air pressure** The downward force caused by the weight of the air pressing on the surface of Earth.

**anticyclone** A large system of high air pressure.

**atmosphere** The layer of gases surrounding Earth.

**blocking high** An area of high pressure that stays in the same place for a long time, preventing other weather systems from moving in.

**cardiovascular system** The body system that includes the heart and blood vessels.

**climate** The average weather in an area over a period of time.

**climatologist** A person who studies the climate.

**dehydration** A potentially dangerous condition caused by a loss of fluids from the body.

**derecho** A widespread, violent windstorm caused by severe thunderstorms.

**desert** A hot, barren region that receives very little rainfall.

**diabetes** A disease that disrupts the body's ability to process a type of sugar called glucose.

**drought** A long period of unusually dry weather.

**dust storm** A strong wind that carries fine particles of earthy material for long distances.

**earthquake** Shaking of the ground caused by the sudden movement of underground rock.

**environmentalist** A person who is concerned about and acts to protect the natural environment.

**evaporate** To change from a liquid into vapor.

**flood** An overflow of water that covers land that is usually dry.

**fossil fuel** A fuel (such as coal, oil, and natural gas) that forms from the remains of prehistoric plants and animals.

**global warming** The gradual warming of Earth's atmosphere over many years.

**greenhouse effect** The warming of the lower atmosphere and surface of a planet by a complex process involving sunlight, gases, and particles in the atmosphere. On Earth, the greenhouse effect began long before human beings existed. However, recent human activity may have added to the effect.

**greenhouse gas** A gas that traps heat in Earth's atmosphere, contributing to global warming.

**habitat** The place in which a plant or animal usually lives.

**heat cramp** Muscle cramp caused by loss of salt and water through sweating.

**heat exhaustion** A condition of weakness caused by exposure to extreme heat.

**heat index** A measure of how hot the air feels to people when moisture is added to the air temperature.

**heat island** An area (such as a city) that has a higher temperature than its surrounding region.

**heat stroke** A serious illness caused by exposure to too much heat.

**high blood pressure** A disease in which the force of a person's blood against the inner walls of the arteries is too high.

**humidity** The amount of moisture (water vapor) in the air.

**hurricane** A tropical storm over the North Atlantic Ocean, the Caribbean Sea, the Gulf of Mexico, or the Northeast Pacific Ocean.

**hydroelectric** Describes the production of electricity from flowing water.

**hyperthermia** A condition that occurs when the body becomes overheated.

**low blood pressure** A condition in which a person's blood pressure has fallen below normal, sometimes causing dizziness, fainting, or in extreme cases, shock.

**malaria** A disease caused by parasites called *Plasmodia,* which are spread through the bite of the *Anopheles* mosquito. Malaria causes a high fever, headache, muscle pain, and nausea, and can be fatal.

**meteorologist** A scientist who studies and forecasts weather.

**monsoon** A wind that reverses itself seasonally, especially the one that blows across the Indian Ocean and surrounding land areas.

**morgue** A place in which medical authorities store the bodies of people who are unidentified or who were killed by accident or violence until they have been identified or the cause of death has been investigated.

**nuclear power reactor** Equipment for producing nuclear energy.

**paleoclimatologists** Scientists who study the climate of prehistoric times.

**perspiration** Sweat—moisture that comes out through the pores of the skin to cool the body.

**pollution** Contamination of the air by industrial waste gases, fuel exhaust, or smoke.

**relative humidity** The amount of water vapor in the air compared with the total amount the air can hold.

**thermometer** An instrument for measuring temperature.

**tinder** Dry wood and other material that catches fire easily.

**tornado** A rapidly rotating column of air that forms under a thundercloud or a developing thundercloud.

**tropical cyclone** A violent storm that starts in the tropics and is made up of winds swirling around an area of low pressure.

**tropics** Regions of Earth that lie within about 1,600 miles (2,580 kilometers) north and south of the equator.

**water vapor** Water in the form of a gas.

**weather system** A particular set of weather conditions in Earth's atmosphere that affects a certain area or region for a time.

**wildfire** An uncontrolled fire on open land (especially a forest fire) that endangers lives and property.

## BOOKS

*Disaster Alert: Drought and Heat Wave Alert,* by Paul Challen, Crabtree, 2004.

*Turbulent Planet: Heat Hazard—Droughts,* by Claire Watts, Raintree, 2004.

*What if We Do Nothing?—Global Warming,* by Neil Morris, Watts, 2007.

*Wild Weather: Heat Wave,* by Catherine Chambers, Heinemann Library, revised ed., 2007.

## WEB SITES

http://www.bbc.co.uk/weather/world/features/sun_know_how.shtml

http://www.fema.gov/areyouready/heat.shtm

http://www.isse.ucar.edu/heat/index.html

http://www.magazine.noaa.gov/stories/mag208.htm

http://www.nws.noaa.gov/om//brochures/heat_wave.shtml

http://www.nws.noaa.gov/om/heat/index.shtml

http://www.weather.com/ready/heat/

http://www.who.int/mediacentre/factsheets/who271/en/

# INDEX